FEAR NOT, CHEER UP, DO NOT DESPAIR

Fear Not, Cheer Up, Do Not Despair

Apostle Dr. Victor Adewusi

Apostle Dr. Victor Adewusi Foundation

Contents

Foreword — vii

1. Be Encouraged — 1
2. Why Must I go Through This? — 5
3. Shades of Trials and Their Effects on us — 10
4. God Will Always Test You — 25
5. Why Must I Cheer up? — 35
6. Major Causes of Despair — 42
7. Fear Demystified — 46
8. What Must we do? — 51
9. Final Antidotes & Nuggets for Fear — 55
10. Why Must we Cheer up? — 58

A Sinner's Prayer — 63
About the Author — 65

Copyright © 2022 by Aposle Dr. Victor Adewusi

All rights reserved. No part of this book may be used or reproduced by any means, graphics, electronic, or mechanical, including photocopying, recording, taping or by any information storage retrieval system without the author's written permission except in cases of brief quotations embodied in critical articles and reviews.

Scripture quotations marked NLT are taken from the New Living Translation. Copyright © 1996, 2004, 2007 by Tyndale House Foundation. Used by permission of Tyndale House Publishers, Inc., Carol Stream, Illinois 60188. All rights reserved.

Author: Apostle Dr. Victor Adewusi

ISBN: 978-1-989099-20-9 (hardcover)
ISBN: 978-1-989099-21-6 (ebook)

First Printing, 2022

Foreword

It is a great honour to write the foreword for one of five books written by my dad, Apostle Victor Adekunle Adewusi, shortly before his passing on 21 August 2022, just three months shy of his 71st birthday. As someone who was spirit-filled, he undoubtedly knew God was soon coming to take him home, and as a result, he wanted to be well prepared and made every attempt at ensuring that his affairs were in order. Therefore, instead of vacationing as he ought to be, he worked feverishly to complete five teaching books to provide practical tools and advice for practically everyone at different phases of their lives. At the time, we all did not understand why he was spending sleepless nights working on completing the books and enduring months of neck pain. We all felt he had lots of time left in this world and kept telling him to save the book writing for later and enjoy his birthday trip. Alas, that was not to be. So it is my prayer that as you pick up each of the books, you will be mightily blessed through them.

Growing up with my dad was an experience I would not trade for the world. Of course, like most kids, I did not cherish the training we had to endure at the time. But looking back now, they have made me the person I am today. My dad always made sure he kept a cheerful attitude when humanly possible. Do not get me wrong; he was human and also had his moments. But, whenever that happened, he "feared not, and cheered up," and as a result, it was difficult to catch him wallowing in despair for long periods of time.

There was a period in our lives that, unbeknownst to most people, was financially tough for our family. Yet, not one of us missed a day of school and neither did we go hungry. Our needs were still met, and life went on as usual, perhaps even better. What was even more surprising during that time was that daddy's countenance never dragged on for long. It would have been understandable if he got angry easily, was short-tempered or even succumbed to depression; however, he made it a point to not wallow in feelings of despair and turned to God for encouragement whenever he was feeling down. It was not until I was much older that I truly realized the magnitude of the trials we went through during that period and gave thanks to God for keeping our family intact.

Anyone who has had the privilege to sit through Lagos traffic will understand that it is difficult to remain pleasant after hours of sitting in traffic, yet that was how daddy operated. Anytime I or my siblings called him, daddy never let his irritation show and rather always sounded like he just got out of a very relaxing massage! That was the kind of person he was. When I went to Lagos for his funeral and experienced Lagos traffic for half a day, I already found myself getting irritated and cranky. But after thinking about the fact that daddy dealt with all this and managed to maintain an upbeat attitude, I was very humbled.

The teaching and tips in this book are ones that I always endeavour to incorporate into my life and teach my family. And I have to say that they have served me well. I recall several times in my adult life when I could have easily let whatever I was going through weigh me down. But by the Grace of God through daddy, I was able to conquer them. Not too long ago, I spoke with someone trained to help families cope with stress, where we discussed the different stressors in my life, and he asked what I did to get through them. I simply explained that I made every effort to ensure that I didn't wallow in feelings of despair for long. Once I acknowledged that I was feeling troubled, I would turn to my faith and to the Bible to help find tools to get myself back up. And of course, my family plays a big role in that as well. When I was done, he was simply amazed. Prior to that point, I had never stopped to think deeply about how I was able to get through difficult situations. Sure, in the back of my mind, I always knew my faith played a big role in how I was able to deal with things. But until that moment, I never truly realized how lucky I was to have been raised by parents that practiced what they preached. If my dad said, "Fear Not, Cheer up, Do Not Despair," you can best believe he was saying it with a cheerful attitude and was not in despair.

Everyone needs to read this book, both young and old, because no one is immune to succumbing to depression regardless of age. Life happens when you least expect it, and by equipping yourself with the tools outlined in the book, you will be able to beat the enemy at his own game.

It is my hope that whenever life's worries weigh you down, and you find yourself fearful of what tomorrow brings, the tips outlined in this book will help you bounce back and live a more cheerful and vibrant life.

Happy Reading, and pick one up for a friend!

Victoria Adetokunbo Adewusi

1

Be Encouraged

With the way many people are committing suicide, deliberately wreaking havoc here and there, and the negative impact of global economies on the lives of citizens of most countries of the world, there has been a great inspiration to write this book.

Undoubtedly, a careful analysis of the performance of many countries' economies in the last ten years shows that their Gross Domestic Product (GDP) is regularly dropping. The price of crude oil is not stable, and for countries with few sources of revenue, creating jobs could be difficult, if not absolutely impossible. However, for some countries that are largely mono-economy, such as Nigeria, the rate of unemployment will definitely continue to be on the decline.

The situation is further exacerbated if any of the countries referred to above do not have resources for large production that could earn them glaring exports to boost their foreign exchange. This matter could become aggravated if such countries depend largely on imports for their consumption instead of encouraging or engaging in local production to serve the basic everyday needs of the people.

With the scenario painted above coupled with dwindling local resources, employment by relevant government agencies and authorities can become drastically reduced. This often leads to job losses due to cuts in staff strength, dismissals, or outright shutdown of both personal and government establishments.

Once a semblance of the above situation becomes apparent, those that were once gainfully employed resort to any or all of the following, among others:

1. **Undue anger**
2. **Unimaginable malice**
3. **Easy provocation**
4. **Increase in crime rates or social vices**
5. **Seclusion**
6. **Attempts to cut corners**
7. **Unrestricted attempts to look for alternative sources of income even if it is to the detriment of their lives**
8. **Shelved responsibilities**
9. **Loss of lives, primarily due to attempted or actual suicides**

Many people do not realize or agree that once in a while in their lives, challenges or issues could arise due to one reason or the other.

Does the Bible say anything about challenges, trials, situations, trying occasions, unexpected issues, or circumstances that we will face as Christians? The answer is "yes," as detailed hereafter, Hebrews 12:7, *"If you endure chastening, God deals with you as with sons; for what son is there whom a father does not chasten?"*

As our ever-loving and caring father, God can decide to chide us whenever we attempt to commit sins or disregard any of His statutes.

Even as earthly fathers and mothers, we can never open our eyes wide and allow our children to go astray without doing everything humanly possible to chide them onto the right path.

The above scripture is also supported by the contents of 1 Thessalonians 3:3, which says, *"That no one should be shaken by these afflictions: for you yourselves know that we are appointed to this."*

Even in Peter's 1st Epistle, Chapter 4, Verse 12 says, *"Beloved, do NOT (emphasis, mine) think it strange concerning the fiery trial which is to try you, as though some strange thing happened to you..."* We certainly cannot claim to be God's "beloved" and expect that things will always be rosy for us in all aspects of our lives or that we won't go through some challenges, as revealed in James 1:2, *"Count it all joy, my brothers, when you meet trials of various kinds."*

From Genesis to Revelation, the Bible is replete with pungent references, which confirm that we are bound to literally "pass through the fire" at some time or the other. Some of them are:

1. **Proverbs 3:11-12** - *"Whom the Lord loveth, He corrected."*
2. **Hebrews 12:5-12** - *"Whom the Lord loveth, He chastened."*
3. **Revelations 3:19** - *"As many as I love, I rebuke and chasten. Therefore be zealous and repent."*
4. **Job 1:21** – *"The Lord gave and the Lord has taken; blessed be His holy name."* The reference is very apt when we remember Job as a man after God's heart. Irrespective of his sinless nature and despite being God's anointed friend, God still allowed Satan to tempt him under the one condition of his life being preserved.
5. **Psalm 34:19** – *"Many are the afflictions of the righteous, But the Lord delivers him out of them all."*

6. **Acts of the Apostles 14:22** – *"...strengthening the souls of the disciples, exhorting them to continue in the faith, and saying, 'We must through many tribulations enter the kingdom of God.'"*
7. **Deuteronomy 8:5** – *"You should know in your heart that as a man chastens his son, so the Lord your God chastens you."*
8. **Matthew 5:4** – *"Blessed are those who mourn, for they shall be comforted."*
9. **1 Peter 5:10** – *"But may the God of all grace, who called us to His eternal glory by Christ Jesus, after you have suffered a while, perfect, establish, strengthen, and settle you."*

Oftentimes, many mortals behave as if they are "on their own." They fail to realize that there is an Almighty God, who is also an Omnipotent Father, an Omnipresent Being, and an Omniscient Creator of the whole universe, who is to be revered. To checkmate us as it were, God can decide to test our loyalty to Him, our love for Him, our faith in Him, our dependence on Him, and our unflinching steadfastness, without any prior notice or permission before He goes ahead to "show himself strong in our lives."

The next chapter will attempt to briefly explain why God allows us to be tested, whether "rightly" or "wrongly."

2

Why Must I go Through This?

As mere mortals with imperfections and an Adamic nature, we commit sins either deliberately or inadvertently; so, no human being can therefore claim to be perfect in the presence of God.

Among the whites and the blacks worldwide, the former seems to be prevalent- that is, we commit sin deliberately more than we do accidentally.

And because God said that no sinner shall go unpunished, we are bound to pay for our sins, whether we like it or not. Conversely, God, in his unquestionable capacity, can, at any time, decide to put us on the line without committing any sin whatsoever.

Some of the reasons "why" and "how" God allows us to be dealt with are narrated with the following explanations:

1. In all that He allows to happen, He remains just, according to **Nehemiah 9:33** – *"Thou art just in all that is brought upon us."*

2. **Psalm 19:9b** – "...*the judgements of the Lord are true and righteous.*"
3. **Jeremiah 17:10** - "*I, the Lord search the heart to give every man according to the fruit of his doings.*" is a very piercing reference.

Ezekiel 14:22-23 equally corroborates the preceding explanations, which says, *"Yet behold, there shall be left in it a remnant who will be brought out, both sons and daughters; surely they will come out to you, and you will see their ways and their doings. Then you will be comforted concerning the disaster that I have brought upon Jerusalem, all that I have brought upon it. And they will comfort you, when you see their ways and their doings; and you shall know that I have done nothing without cause that I have done in it,' says the Lord God."*

Whenever we deliberately go against God's commandments and statutes, we should be ready to pay for that act of sin and disobedience. In Isaiah 66:4, God states the consequences for acts of deliberate disobedience *"So, I will choose their delusions, and bring their fears on them; because they did evil before My eyes, and chose that in which I do not delight."* These consequences are also backed by Genesis 42:21, "*We are guilty, therefore is distress come upon us.*"

In some instances, God wants to confirm the genuineness of our love for Him. Is the love lukewarm, total, or not in place at all?

Our allegiance to Him must be total, not half measured. Our affection for him must be seen to be obviously unrivalled, beyond and above the one that exists between families or pairs of any form or nature.

At every point in time, our mind, heart and actions must reflect the contents of Psalm 73:25, which says, "*Whom have I in heaven but Thee, and there is none upon the earth that I desire beside Thee.*" It is the same expectation that he wants us to constantly demonstrate, as shown by king David in the book of Psalms 142:4-5, *"Look on my right hand and see, For there is no one who acknowledges me; Refuge has failed me; No one cares for my soul. I cried out to You, O Lord: I said, "You are my refuge, my portion in the land of the living."*

Whenever we are going through troubled waters, He wants us to be able to boldly declare and refer to Isaiah 54:1 & 5-6, which is paraphrased thus: *"Sing for the Maker is thine husband, the Lord hath called thee as a woman forsaken."*

Therefore, from the foregoing, our heavenly Father can, without our moral permission, suddenly "emerge" as He pleases to challenge and test our faith. Some people taste their own very early in life, others in the middle of their lives, while the majority would have their own experience towards the tail end of their sojourn on earth; but regardless of when we do, we surely cannot escape it! What's more? We dare not complain nor query Him because He does as He wishes, as in Psalm 115:3, *"But our God is in heaven; He does whatever He pleases."*

Brethren since He has given us His assurance in John 14:18 that He will not leave us comfortless, but come to us and see us through, then we, as children of God, must be ready and willingly prepared to be tested by Him at any point in our lives.

He also says in Proverbs 3:5 that we should trust in the Lord but lean NOT on our own understanding. His ways also differ from ours; hence nobody has the moral right to query Him as buttressed by Isaiah 55:8-9, which says, *"For My thoughts are not your thoughts, Nor are your ways My ways,"* says the Lord. *"For as the heavens are higher than the earth, so are My ways higher than your ways, And My thoughts than your thoughts."*

In the 25th verse of the 5th chapter of his write-up, Prophet Jeremiah clearly states that *"your sins have withheld good things from you."* Thus, to emphasize, we can be chastised by God because of our sins or because He just wants to demonstrate His unquestionable nature towards us. If we take a cursory look into the Biblical account during the destruction of Jerusalem, God knew what He was doing when He decided to ensure that Jeremiah spent a longer time in prison. He extended his stay in prison to keep him safe from being killed or harmed, according to Jeremiah 37:15-16 and 39:11-14.

All things work together for good to those who love Him and are called according to His purpose (Romans 8:28). A clear example of this is when God demonstrated His love and affection for Joseph by allowing his brothers to sell him into slavery. By the time Joseph's brothers went to Egypt during the famine in Israel, they could not recognize Joseph again. He was forced to say, "*Ye thought evil against me, but God meant it on to good.*" (Genesis 50:20) Joseph learned one of God's statutes, that it was good that he was afflicted, based on the contents of David's book of Psalms, chapter 119:17, *"Deal bountifully with Your servant, That I may live and keep Your word."*

It is worth emphasizing here that we must endeavour as much as possible to keep God's commandments in our hearts as a matter of compulsion. The Bible is very concise; as mentioned in Genesis 41:21, He can openly punish us once we commit an offence. In his book of Psalms, chapter 31:9-10, King David says, "*Have mercy on me, O Lord, for I am in trouble; My eye wastes away with grief, Yes, my soul and my body! For my life is spent with grief, and my years with sighing; My strength fails because of my iniquity, And my bones waste away.*" The same is underscored in the 38th chapter of Psalms, verses 1-8, wherein David said that there was no soundness in his flesh because of the numerous sins that he had committed.

As much as we can, we should also strive to adhere to God's words and commandments in order to openly avoid the contents of:

1. **Psalm 89:30-32** - *"If his sons forsake My law And do not walk in My judgments, If they break My statutes And do not keep My commandments, Then I will punish their transgression with the rod, And their iniquity with stripes..."*
2. **Psalm 78:32-33** - *"In spite of this they still sinned, And did not believe in His wondrous works. Therefore their days He consumed in futility, And their years in fear."*
3. **Deuteronomy 11:28** - *"...and the curse, if you do not obey the commandments of the Lord your God, but turn aside from the way which I command you today, to go after other gods which you have not know."*

The next chapter will attempt to focus on the types of challenges that we usually go through and their impacts on our lives.

3

Shades of Trials and Their Effects on us

There are usually at least two sides to everything in life, which is why I wish to categorically state that we, at the very least, have two *shades* of trials, which is what this chapter will focus on.

The two shades are:

1. **Trials, challenges, or situations brought upon us by ourselves which are self-inflicted.**
2. **Trails, challenges, or situations that come directly from God. Yes, from God!**

The first aspect is biblically backed up by Deuteronomy 28:20, which says, *"The Lord will send on you cursing, confusion, and rebuke in all that you set your hand to do, until you are destroyed and until you perish quickly, because of the wickedness of your doings in which you have forsaken Me."*

Also, according to the same book (Deuteronomy 28:15-67), a series of negative consequences await whoever decides to shun the ways of the Lord. On the contrary, verses 1 to 14 of the same chapter are filled with blessings, prayers and positive expectations for whoever walks diligently within His tenets, laws and statutes.

Many people were born as wicked beings; hence they perpetrate evil all the days of their lives. In their sight, they see devilish acts as good deeds, without minding whose ox is gored or the consequences therefrom.

Job 15:20a is more apt when we talk about what awaits the wicked man as a reward. It says, *"The wicked man writhes with pain all his days..."*

Psalm 32:10a - *"Many sorrows shall be to the wicked..."*

Isaiah 57:20-21 - *"But the wicked are like the troubled sea, When it cannot rest, whose waters cast up mire and dirt. 'There is no peace,' Says my God, 'for the wicked."*

Furthermore, since some people have dedicated themselves to perpetuating evil and disobeying God's doctrines, the consequences of their actions and behaviours will have dire repercussions as backed by Isaiah 42:24-25, which says, *"Who gave Jacob for a spoil, and Israel to the robbers? Did not the Lord, He against whom we have sinned? For they would not walk in His ways, neither were they obedient unto his law. Therefore He hath poured upon him the fury of His anger, and the strength of battle..."*

Remember, we are still talking about the shades of trials that human beings go through, and I said that there are two: those that are self-inflicted and those that come directly from God.

Let us briefly discuss other aspects of the self-inflicted ones, as exemplified in:

1. **1 Corinthians 3:17** – *"If any man defiles his body, him shall God destroy."*
2. **Proverbs 23:29-35** talks at length regarding drug abuse and alcoholism plus other worldly abuses, which could cause significant discomfort to the human body. Many people are simply unable to control their eating habits; they are ever ready and willing to devour whatever comes their way as a way of life or means of enjoyment!
3. **Numbers 11:19-20** also says, *"Ye shall not eat one day, nor two days, nor five days, neither ten days, nor twenty days; But even a whole month, until it come out at your nostrils, and it be loathsome unto you: because that ye have despised the Lord which is among you, and have wept before Him, saying, Why came we forth out of Egypt?"*

Another major source of self-adjudged suffering is sexual perversion by both men and women. Many of us tend to overlook and forget that Lord said our body is His temple and must not be defiled or debased by inordinate or wanton sex escapades, based on Romans 1:27, *"And likewise also the men, leaving the natural use of the woman, burned in their lust one toward another; men with men working that which is unseemly, and receiving in themselves that recompense of their error which was meet."* Today, many men and women are glaringly backward spiritually, financially, morally, and even psychologically as a result of insincerity and infidelity toward their spouses. Undoubtedly, God does not authorize this act, but man brings any discomfort that arises therefrom by himself.

It is also worthy to note that physical and environmental factors play significant roles in our day-to-day activities, particularly welfare. Many people are less bothered about cleanliness, which they say is next to godliness. For some, their daily environment is loaded and surrounded by filth without concern; and can be comparable to pigs. Come to think of it; God is very particular about our environment, which is attested by the following biblical references:

1. **Zephaniah 3:1** – *"Woe to her that is filthy and polluted, to the oppressing city!"*
2. **Jeremiah 2:7** – *"I brought you into a bountiful country, to eat its fruit and its goodness. But when you entered, you defiled My land And made My heritage an abomination."*
3. **Revelations 11:18b** – *"...And that You should reward Your servants the prophets and the saints, And those who fear Your name, small and great, And should destroy those who destroy the earth."*
4. **Micah 2:10b** – *"...Because it is defiled, it shall destroy, yes, with utter destruction."*
5. **Isaiah 24:5** – *"The earth is also defiled under its inhabitants, because they have transgressed the laws, Changed the ordinance, Broken the everlasting covenant."* Some major factors that cause or bring challenges to people's lives are greed and oppression, necessitated by covetousness, insincerity, and by robbing Peter to pay Paul. For instance, Achan's covetousness caused many Israelites to die as recorded in **Joshua 7:1-26**, *But the children of Israel committed a trespass in the accursed thing: for Achan, the son of Carmi, the son of Zabdi, the son of Zerah, of the tribe of Judah, took of the accursed thing: and the anger of the Lord was kindled against the children of Israel. Now Joshua sent men from Jericho to Ai, which is beside Beth Aven, on the east side of Bethel, and spoke to them, saying, "Go up and spy out the country." So the men went up and spied out Ai. And they returned to Joshua and said to him, "Do not let all the people go up, but let about two or three thousand men go up and attack Ai. Do not weary all the people there, for the people of Ai are few." So about three thousand men went up there from the people, but they fled before the men of Ai. And the men of Ai struck down about thirty-six*

men, for they chased them from before the gate as far as Shebarim, and struck them down on the descent; therefore the hearts of the people melted and became like water. Then Joshua tore his clothes, and fell to the earth on his face before the ark of the Lord until evening, he and the elders of Israel; and they put dust on their heads. And Joshua said, "Alas, Lord God, why have You brought this people over the Jordan at all—to deliver us into the hand of the Amorites, to destroy us? Oh, that we had been content, and dwelt on the other side of the Jordan! O Lord, what shall I say when Israel turns its back before its enemies? For the Canaanites and all the inhabitants of the land will hear it, and surround us, and cut off our name from the earth. Then what will You do for Your great name?" So the Lord said to Joshua: "Get up! Why do you lie thus on your face? Israel has sinned, and they have also transgressed My covenant which I commanded them. For they have even taken some of the accursed things, and have both stolen and deceived, and they have also put it among their own stuff. Therefore the children of Israel could not stand before their enemies, but turned their backs before their enemies, because they have become doomed to destruction. Neither will I be with you anymore, unless you destroy the accursed from among you. Get up, sanctify the people, and say, 'Sanctify yourselves for tomorrow, because thus says the Lord God of Israel: "There is an accursed thing in your midst, O Israel; you cannot stand before your enemies until you take away the accursed thing from among you." In the morning therefore you shall be brought according to your tribes. And it shall be that the tribe which the Lord takes shall come according to families; and the family which the Lord takes shall come by households; and the household which the Lord takes shall come man by man. Then it shall be that he who is taken with the accursed thing shall be burned with fire, he and all that he has, because he has transgressed the covenant of the Lord, and because he has done a disgraceful thing in Israel.'" So Joshua rose early in the morning and brought Israel by their tribes, and the tribe of Judah was taken. He brought the clan of Judah, and he took the family of the Zarhites; and he brought the family of the Zarhites man by man, and Zabdi was taken. Then he brought his household man by man, and Achan the son of Carmi, the son of Zabdi, the son of Zerah, of the tribe of Judah, was taken. Now Joshua said to Achan, "My son, I beg you, give glory to the Lord God of Israel, and make confession to Him, and tell me now what you have done; do not hide it from me." And Achan answered Joshua and said, "Indeed I have sinned against the Lord God of Israel, and this is what I have done: When I saw among the spoils a beautiful Babylonian garment, two hundred shekels of silver, and a wedge of gold weighing fifty shekels, I coveted them and took them. And there they are, hidden in the earth in the midst of my tent, with the silver under it." So Joshua sent messengers, and they ran to the tent; and there it was, hidden in his tent, with the silver under it. And they took them from the midst of the tent, brought them to Joshua and to all the children of Israel, and laid them out before the Lord. Then Joshua, and all Israel with him, took Achan the son of Zerah, the silver, the garment, the wedge of gold, his sons, his daughters, his oxen, his donkeys, his sheep, his tent, and all that he had, and they brought them to the Valley of Achor. And Joshua said, "Why have you troubled us? The Lord will trouble you this day." So all Israel stoned him with stones; and they burned them with fire after they had stoned them with stones. Then they raised over him a great heap of stones, still there to this day. So the Lord turned from the fierceness of His anger. Therefore the name of that place has been called the Valley of Achor to this day.

6. **Proverbs 15:27** corroborates the above, *"He who is greedy for gain troubles his own house, but he who hates bribes will live."*

Challenges Known by God

Many people do not know, believe or agree that God can allow us to experience different challenges; for reasons best known to Him. Some of which are highlighted below:

1. God always wants to draw us closer to Him. According to **Psalm 107:13**, *"Then they cried out to the Lord in their trouble, And He saved them out of their distresses."*
2. He also always wants to ascertain the contents of our hearts and know how faithful we are to Him because **Exodus 20:20** says, *"And Moses said unto the people, 'Fear not: for God is come to prove you, and that His fear may be before your faces, that ye sin not.'"*
3. **Deuteronomy 8:2** confirms the above point by saying that the Lord *"tested you to know what was in thine heart."*
4. *"I, the Lord, search the heart to give every man according to his way and the fruit of his doings."* (**Jeremiah 17:10**)
5. **Deuteronomy 13:3-4** testifies to it thus, *"...you shall not listen to the words of that prophet or that dreamer of dreams, for the Lord your God is testing you to know whether you love the Lord your God with all your heart and with all your soul. You shall walk after the Lord your God and fear Him, and keep His commandments and obey His voice; you shall serve Him and hold fast to Him."*

As our ultimate Creator, God will always want to draw us closer to His word, according to Psalm 94:12, *"Blessed is the man whom You instruct, O Lord, And teach out of Your law..."* and Psalm 119:71, *"It is good for me that I have been afflicted, that I may learn Your statutes."*

God also wants us to be openly obedient to Him based on Hebrews 5:8, *"Though He were a son, yet learned He obedience by the things which He* suffered." Please also refer to Hebrews 2:10, *For it became Him, for whom are all things, and by whom are all things, in bringing many sons unto glory, to make the captain of their salvation perfect through sufferings.*

As benevolent as God is, He is ever willing to make us a better and more useful vessel at all times because of His unflinching love for us, as clearly shown in the two following scriptures:

1. **Jeremiah 18:4** – *"And the vessel that He made of clay was marred in the hand of the potter: so He made it again another vessel, as seemed good to the potter to make it."*
2. **1 Corinthians 5:7** – *"Purge out therefore the old leaven, that ye may be a new lump, as ye are unleavened. For even Christ our Passover is sacrificed for us…"*

Our Almighty Father is also ever willing to purify us just as a precious metal is refined based on these Biblical references:

1. **Micah 3:3** – *"Who also eat the flesh of My people, Flay their skin from them, Break their bones, And chop them in pieces Like meat for the pot, Like flesh in the caldron."*
2. **Zechariah 13:9a** – *"I will bring the one-third through the fire, Will refine them as silver is refined, and test them as gold is tested…"*
3. **Job 23:10** - *"But He knows the way that I take; When He has tested me, I shall come forth as gold."*
4. **Psalm 73:17** – *"… until I went into the sanctuary of God; then I understood their end."*
5. **Acts 19:26** – *"Moreover you see and hear that not only at Ephesus, but throughout almost all Asia, this Paul has persuaded and turned away many people, saying that they are not gods which are made with hands."*

6. **Isaiah 48:10** – *"Behold, I have refined you, but not as silver; I have tested you in the furnace of affliction."*
7. **1 Peter 1:7** – *"... that the genuineness of your faith, being much more precious than gold that perishes, though it is tested by fire, may be found to praise, honor, and glory at the revelation of Jesus Christ..."*

If we consider the life of Joseph, we will agree that for man to have a lasting testimony that can serve as a verifiable lesson to others, they must be thoroughly tested and tried. And what's more? The reward is usually bountiful, as revealed in Joseph's life in (Genesis 37 – 42), but equally succinctly supported by Psalm 66:12, *"You have caused men to ride over our heads; we went through fire and through water; but You brought us out to rich fulfillment."* And also, James 5:11, which says, *"Indeed we count them blessed who endure. You have heard of the perseverance of Job and seen the end intended by the Lord – that the Lord is very compassionate and merciful."*

The same goes for Job 42:10-17, and I quote, *"And the Lord turned the captivity of Job, when he prayed for his friends: also the Lord gave Job twice as much as he had before. Then came there unto him all his brethren, and all his sisters, and all they that had been of his acquaintance before, and did eat bread with him in his house: and they bemoaned him, and comforted him over all the evil that the Lord had brought upon him: every man also gave him a piece of money, and every one an earring of gold. So the Lord blessed the latter end of Job more than his beginning: for he had fourteen thousand sheep, and six thousand camels, and a thousand yoke of oxen, and a thousand she asses. He had also seven sons and three daughters. And he called the name of the first, Jemima; and the name of the second, Kezia; and the name of the third, Keren–happuch. And in all the land were no women found so fair as the daughters of Job: and their father gave them inheritance among their brethren. After this* lived Job a hundred and forty years, and saw his sons, and his sons' sons, even four generations. So Job died, being old and full of days."

According to **Romans 8:18**, *"For I reckon that the sufferings of this present time are not worthy to be compared with the glory which shall be revealed in us."* This shows that whoever endures temptations without grumbling stands to become blessed at the end of the day as it relates to challenges and trials.

James 1:12 says, *"But above all, my brethren, do not swear, either by heaven or by earth or with any other oath. But let your 'yes' be 'yes,' and your 'no,' 'no,' lest you fall into judgment."*

1 Peter 4:13 - *"... but rejoice to the extent that you partake of Christ's sufferings, that when His glory is revealed, you may also be glad with exceeding joy."*

In **Deuteronomy 8:16**, the Bible says, *"... who fed you in the wilderness with manna, which your fathers did not know, that He might humble you and that He might test you, to do you good in the end"*

In **Psalm 105:17-22**, we read the account of how Joseph was imprisoned, abased, and tested before he was exalted: *"He sent a man before them— Joseph— who was sold as a slave. They hurt his feet with fetters, He was laid in irons. Until the time that his word came to pass, The word of the Lord tested him. The king sent and released him, The ruler of the people let him go free. He made him Lord of his house, And ruler of all his possessions, To bind his princes at his pleasure, And teach his elders wisdom."*

Proverbs 18:12b - *"...and before honor is humility."*

The above passages show that God can deliberately orchestrate challenges before allowing us to receive blessings, positions, and exalted ministries. It is said that nothing good comes easy and nothing ventured is nothing gained. A gold bracelet is unavoidably incomplete unless it passes through fire. And it is quite apt because some people do not appreciate what they have unless they suffer or strive for it immensely. Man can, unavoidably, suffer for his impenitent sins in his heart as revealed in Jeremiah 5:25, and I quote, *"Your iniquities have turned away these things and your sins have withholden good things from you."*

Many people usually think and conclude within their minds that, at times, God does not want to answer their prayer requests or grant them their hearts' desires, which is extremely incorrect. Oftentimes, the reason for unanswered prayers could be found in James 4:2-3, which says, *"You lust and do not have. You murder and covet and cannot obtain. You fight and war. Yet you do not have because you do not ask. You ask and do not receive, because you ask amiss, that you may spend it on your pleasures,"* meaning we seldom ask Him with the wrong motives!

On the other hand, God may decide to withhold that which you earnestly desire or expect because He has something better to offer you! We can confirm this in Psalm 81:10-13, which says, *"I am the Lord your God, Who brought you out of the land of Egypt; Open your mouth wide, and I will fill it. But My people would not heed My voice, And Israel would have none of Me. So I gave them over to their own stubborn heart, To walk in their own counsels. Oh, that My people would listen to Me, That Israel would walk in My ways,"* and verse 16 thus, *"He would have fed them also with the finest of wheat; And with honey from the rock I would have satisfied you."*

God seriously warns us to avoid insisting on having our way at all costs in order to avoid His unwarranted wrath! Check out the following scriptures to back it up:

1. **Psalm 78:27-31** - *"He also rained meat on them like the dust, Feathered fowl like the sand of the seas; And He let them fall in the midst of their camp, All around their dwellings. So they ate and were well filled, For He gave them their own desire. They were not deprived of their craving; But while their food was still in their mouths, The wrath of God came against them, And slew the stoutest of them, And struck down the choice men of Israel."*

2. **Psalm 106:14-15** - *"But lusted exceedingly in the wilderness, And tested God in the desert. And He gave them their request, But sent leanness into their soul."*

3. **Numbers 11:4-34** - *"Now the mixed multitude who were among them yielded to intense craving; so the children of Israel also wept again and said: "Who will give us meat to eat? We remember the fish which we ate freely in Egypt, the cucumbers, the melons, the leeks, the onions, and the garlic; but now our whole being is dried up; there is nothing at all except this manna before our eyes!" Now the manna was like coriander seed, and its color like the color of bdellium. The people went about and gathered it, ground it on millstones or beat it in the mortar, cooked it in pans, and made cakes of it; and its taste was like the taste of pastry prepared with oil. And when the dew fell on the camp in the night, the manna fell on it. Then Moses heard the people weeping throughout their families, everyone at the door of his tent; and the anger of the Lord was greatly aroused; Moses also was displeased. So Moses said to the Lord, "Why have You afflicted Your servant? And why have I not found favor in Your sight, that You have laid the burden of all these people on me? Did I conceive all these people? Did I beget them, that You should say to me,'Carry them in your bosom, as a guardian*

carries a nursing child,' to the land which You swore to their fathers? Where am I to get meat to give to all these people? For they weep all over me, saying, 'Give us meat, that we may eat.' I am not able to bear all these people alone, because the burden is too heavy for me. If You treat me like this, please kill me here and now—if I have found favor in Your sight—and do not let me see my wretchedness!" So the Lord said to Moses: "Gather to Me seventy men of the elders of Israel, whom you know to be the elders of the people and officers over them; bring them to the tabernacle of meeting, that they may stand there with you. Then I will come down and talk with you there. I will take of the Spirit that is upon you and will put the same upon them; and they shall bear the burden of the people with you, that you may not bear it yourself alone. Then you shall say to the people, 'Consecrate yourselves for tomorrow, and you shall eat meat; for you have wept in the hearing of the Lord, saying, "Who will give us meat to eat? For it was well with us in Egypt." Therefore the Lord will give you meat, and you shall eat. You shall eat, not one day, nor two days, nor five days, nor ten days, nor twenty days, but for a whole month, until it comes out of your nostrils and becomes loathsome to you, because you have despised the Lord who is among you, and have wept before Him, saying, "Why did we ever come up out of Egypt?' And Moses said, "The people whom I am among are six hundred thousand men on foot; yet You have said, 'I will give them meat, that they may eat for a whole month.' Shall flocks and herds be slaughtered for them, to provide enough for them? Or shall all the fish of the sea be gathered together for them, to provide enough for them?" And the Lord said to Moses, "Has the Lord's arm been shortened? Now you shall see whether what I say will happen to you or not." So Moses went out and told the people the words of the Lord, and he gathered the seventy men of the elders of the people and placed them around the tabernacle. Then the Lord came down in the cloud, and spoke to him, and took of the Spirit that was upon him, and placed the same upon the seventy elders; and it happened, when the Spirit rested upon them, that they prophesied, although they never did so again. But two men had remained in the camp: the name of one was Eldad, and the name of the other Medad. And the Spirit rested upon them. Now they were among those listed, but who had not gone out to the tabernacle; yet they prophesied in the camp. And a young man ran and told Moses, and said, "Eldad and Medad are prophesying in the camp." So Joshua the son of Nun, Moses' assistant, one of his choice men, answered and said, "Moses my Lord, forbid them!" Then Moses said to him, "Are you zealous for my sake? Oh, that all the Lord's people were prophets and that the Lord would put His Spirit upon them!" And Moses returned to the camp, he and the elders of Israel. Now a wind went out from the Lord, and it brought quail from the sea and left them fluttering near the camp, about a day's journey on this side and about a day's journey on the other side, all around the camp, and about two cubits above the surface of the ground. And the people stayed up all that day, all night, and all the next day, and gathered the quail (he who gathered least gathered ten homers); and they spread them out for themselves all around the camp. But while the meat was still between their teeth, before it was chewed, the wrath of the Lord was aroused against the people, and the Lord struck the people with a very great plague. So he called the name of that place Kibroth Hattaavah, because there they buried the people who had yielded to craving."

It is, however, instructive to mention that if human beings endeavour to sacrifice themselves, deny and endure temptations genuinely, God will usually reward and compensate them at the end of the day. The following Golden Verses support this:

1. **Genesis 22:12** - *"And He said, 'Do not lay your hand on the lad, or do anything to him; for now I know that you fear God, since you have not withheld your son, your only son, from Me.'"*
2. **Hebrews 6:15** – *"And so, after he had patiently endured, he obtained the promise."*

From the above accounts, one can see that while God instructed Abraham to sacrifice his only son, Isaac, He already knew that He would not allow Isaac to be slaughtered. He only wanted to test Abraham's faith to justify that he truly deserved the enormous rewards, blessings, and potential that ultimately awaited him! And lo and behold, God had already provided a replacement for Isaac, even before Abraham got to the place where Isaac was to be sacrificed. However, let me clarify by emphasizing that you can never obtain, execute, or do anything successfully in the physical, unless and until it is activated in the spiritual realm.

In other words, it is emphatic to stress that Abraham had actually "sacrificed" Isaac in the spiritual realm within his heart, as deemed by God, hence the surprise replacement with a ram!

4

God Will Always Test You

There are various reasons why God tests us. He has a lot of great plans for us but wants to confirm that we justify the good things that He has in store for us before releasing the goodies! Some of the reasons, to the best of my knowledge, are listed below:

1. **He wants to ascertain what is in our hearts and how committed we are to Him**
2. **To draw us closer to the constant application and appreciation of His words, the Rhema**
3. **He wants to teach us how to be totally obedient to Him and His statutes, laws and commandments**
4. **To make us better vessels of honour to prepare us for future and greater assignments or positions ahead of the tasks**
5. **He would want to draw us closer to him**
6. **To remove the clogs from our ways to stardom**
7. **He wants us to be able to adapt to challenges**
8. **To prepare us to be compassionate**
9. **To teach us patience, to purify us of our sins and refine us**

10. **He wishes to teach us obedience**
11. **He plans to make us bear more fruit**
12. **To humble us and make us wiser**
13. **He has a loving reason for whatever he does**

There are numerous Biblical references to support the above reasons why God will want to test us to confirm that – indeed – we desire to be called His chosen vessel, to justify the exalted positions that He has for us, to give us victory overseen and unexpected temptations, and to demonstrate to Him that we actually desire His Crown of glory.

I would encourage you to diligently take your time going through the scriptures listed here-under and ponder over them with religious attention, to really gain and assimilate their essence:

1. **Romans 8:25** – *"But if we hope for what we do not see, we eagerly wait for it with perseverance."*
2. **Psalm 119:71** – *"It is good for me that I have been afflicted, That I may learn Your statutes."*
3. **Psalm 78:38-39** – *"But He, being full of compassion, forgave their iniquity, And did not destroy them. Yes, many a time He turned His anger away, And did not stir up all His wrath; For He remembered that they were but flesh, A breath that passes away and does not come again."*
4. **Job 5:6-7** – *"For affliction does not come from the dust, Nor does trouble spring from the ground; Yet man is born to trouble, As the sparks fly upward."*
5. **Psalm 31:9-10** – *"Have mercy on me, O Lord, for I am in trouble; My eye wastes away with grief, Yes, my soul and my body! For my life is spent with grief, And my years with sighing; My strength fails because of my iniquity, And my bones waste away."*

6. **Genesis 3:16-19** – *"To the woman He said: "I will greatly multiply your sorrow and your conception; In pain you shall bring forth children; Your desire shall be for your husband, And he shall rule over you." Then to Adam He said, "Because you have heeded the voice of your wife, and have eaten from the tree of which I commanded you, saying, 'You shall not eat of it': "Cursed is the ground for your sake; In toil you shall eat of it All the days of your life. Both thorns and thistles it shall bring forth for you, And you shall eat the herb of the field. In the sweat of your face you shall eat bread Till you return to the ground, For out of it you were taken; For dust you are, And to dust you shall return."*

7. **Psalm 89:30-32** – *"If his sons forsake My law And do not walk in My judgments, If they break My statutes And do not keep My commandments, Then I will punish their transgression with the rod, And their iniquity with stripes."*

8. **2 Corinthians 11:23-30** – *"Are they ministers of Christ?—I speak as a fool—I am more: in labors more abundant, in stripes above measure, in prisons more frequently, in deaths often. From the Jews five times I received forty stripes minus one. Three times I was beaten with rods; once I was stoned; three times I was shipwrecked; a night and a day I have been in the deep; in journeys often, in perils of waters, in perils of robbers, in perils of my own countrymen, in perils of the Gentiles, in perils in the city, in perils in the wilderness, in perils in the sea, in perils among false brethren; in weariness and toil, in sleeplessness often, in hunger and thirst, in fastings often, in cold and nakedness— besides the other things, what comes upon me daily: my deep concern for all the churches. Who is weak, and I am not weak? Who is made to stumble, and I do not burn with indignation? If I must boast, I will boast in the things which concern my infirmity."*

9. **Philippians 2:27-30** – *"For indeed he was sick almost unto death; but God had mercy on him, and not only on him but on me also,*

lest I should have sorrow upon sorrow. Therefore I sent him the more eagerly, that when you see him again you may rejoice, and I may be less sorrowful. Receive him therefore in the Lord with all gladness, and hold such men in esteem; because for the work of Christ he came close to death, not regarding his life, to supply what was lacking in your service toward me."

10. **Psalm 94:12** – "Blessed is the man whom You instruct, O Lord , And teach out of Your law..."
11. **Psalm 66:10** – "For You, O God, have tested us; You have refined us as silver is refined."
12. **John 15:2** – "Every branch in Me that does not bear fruit He takes away; and every branch that bears fruit He prunes, that it may bear more fruit."
13. **2 Chronicles 33:12** – "Now when he was in affliction, he implored the Lord his God, and humbled himself greatly before the God of his fathers..."
14. **Ecclesiastes 7:2-3** – "Better to go to the house of mourning Than to go to the house of feasting, for that is the end of all men; and the living will take it to heart. Sorrow is better than laughter, for by a sad countenance, the heart is made better."
15. **2 Corinthians 1:4** – "...who comforts us in all our tribulation, that we may be able to comfort those who are in any trouble, with the comfort with which we ourselves are comforted by God."
16. **2 Corinthians 4:17** – "For our light affliction, which is but for a moment, is working for us a far more exceeding and eternal weight of glory..."
17. **Isaiah 53:3-5** – "He is despised and rejected by men, A Man of sorrows and acquainted with grief. And we hid, as it were, our faces from Him; He was despised, and we did not esteem Him. Surely He has borne our griefs and carried our sorrows; yet we esteemed Him stricken, Smitten

by God, and afflicted. But He was wounded for our transgressions, He was bruised for our iniquities; The chastisement for our peace was upon Him, And by His stripes we are healed."

18. **1 Peter 3:18** – *"For Christ also suffered once for sins, the just for the unjust, that He might bring us to God, being put to death in the flesh but made alive by the Spirit..."*

19. **1 Peter 2:21** – *"For to this you were called, because Christ also suffered for us, leaving us an example, that you should follow His steps."*

20. **Philippians 3:8** – *"Yet indeed I also count all things loss for the excellence of the knowledge of Christ Jesus my Lord, for whom I have suffered the loss of all things, and count them as rubbish, that I may gain Christ..."*

21. **Jeremiah 10:19** – *"Woe is me for my hurt! My wound is severe. But I say, 'Truly this is an infirmity, And I must bear it.'"*

22. **Lamentations 3:24-26** – *"The Lord is my portion," says my soul, "Therefore I hope in Him!" The Lord is good to those who wait for Him, to the soul who seeks Him. It is good that one should hope and wait quietly for the salvation of the Lord."*

23. **1 Thessalonians 3:3-4** – *"...that no one should be shaken by these afflictions; for you yourselves know that we are appointed to this. For, in fact, we told you before when we were with you that we would suffer tribulation, just as it happened, and you know."*

24. **1 Peter 4:12-16** – *"Beloved, do not think it strange concerning the fiery trial which is to try you, as though some strange thing happened to you; but rejoice to the extent that you partake of Christ's sufferings, that when His glory is revealed, you may also be glad with exceeding joy. If you are reproached for the name of Christ, blessed are you, for the Spirit of glory and of God rests upon you. On their part He is blasphemed, but on your part He is glorified. But let none of you suffer as a murderer, a thief, an evildoer, or as a busybody in other people's*

matters. Yet if anyone suffers as a Christian, let him not be ashamed, but let him glorify God in this matter."

25. **Psalm 119:143** – *"Trouble and anguish have overtaken me, Yet Your commandments are my delights."*
26. **Hebrews 11:25-27** – *"...choosing rather to suffer affliction with the people of God than to enjoy the passing pleasures of sin, esteeming the reproach of Christ greater riches than the treasures in Egypt; for he looked to the reward. By faith he forsook Egypt, not fearing the wrath of the king; for he endured as seeing Him who is invisible."*
27. **James 5:10-11** – *"My brethren, take the prophets, who spoke in the name of the Lord, as an example of suffering and patience. Indeed we count them blessed who endure. You have heard of the perseverance of Job and seen the end intended by the Lord—that the Lord is very compassionate and merciful."*

A cursory look into all of the above shows a common thread, which is to fashion us after the image of Jesus Christ, Our Lord and personal Savior.

Another scripture reference openly relevant to this chapter and the golden verses referred to above is found in John 16:33. I came across this particular portion at the age of 12, and that is why to this day, I've always had an "open mind" concerning any issue of life that attempts to stare me in the face. Perhaps you, my reader, are even familiar with the Bible passage, but just in case you are not, permit me to state it thus. John 16:33, *"These things I have spoken to you, that in Me you may have peace. In the world you will have tribulation; but be of good cheer, I have overcome the world."*

As Believers, we are not supposed to be slaves to fear. Never. According to Romans 8:15, we did not receive a spirit that makes us afraid, fearful or panic over little or great life issues. According to 2 Timothy

1:7, our heavenly Father did not give us the spirit of timidity. Instead, He promised us the perfect Spirit of love, power, self-discipline, and unflinching trust in God, the Almighty. I have discovered the following essence in life as a Believer; a genuine and born-again Christian:

1. Once you trust in God with all your might, you will overcome fear or timidity. The Bible says, in **Psalm 56:3-4**, that *"Whenever I am afraid, I will trust in You. In God (I will praise His word), In God I have put my trust; I will not fear. What can flesh do to me?"*
2. It is not good to fear those who can kill the body but who cannot kill the soul; according to **Matthew 10:28**, *"And do not fear those who kill the body but cannot kill the soul. But rather fear Him who is able to destroy both soul and body in hell."*
3. Based on what the greatest psalmist of all times – David – said, God should be the only source of light and freedom to the believer. **Psalm 27:1**, *"The Lord is my light and my salvation; Whom shall I fear? The Lord is the strength of my life; Of whom shall I be afraid?"*
4. Another major reason that would make a child of God constantly fearful is that he indulges in sin.
5. Someone who professes to be a child of God but has other smaller gods they worship or bow down to is most likely expected to be fearful due to an unavoidable guilty conscience.
6. If God is our only Helper, one need not be afraid in any situation; according to **Hebrews 13:5-6**, *"Let your conduct be without covetousness; be content with such things as you have. For He Himself has said, "I will never leave you nor forsake you." So we may boldly say: "The Lord is my helper; I will not fear. What can man do to me?"*
7. In **1 John 4:18**, the Bible says perfect love casts out fear.
8. Once we begin to foresee failure ahead of us, fear becomes unavoidable. Remember when Jesus Christ told Peter to walk on water after seeing Him afar off, standing on the water? He

initially began to walk perfectly well, but the moment Peter began to tremble, he instantly began to sink until Jesus Christ restored his faith, then he began to walk on the water again. **Matthew 14:25-31**, *"Now in the fourth watch of the night Jesus went to them, walking on the sea. And when the disciples saw Him walking on the sea, they were troubled, saying, 'It is a ghost!' And they cried out for fear. But immediately, Jesus spoke to them, saying, 'Be of good cheer! It is I; do not be afraid.' And Peter answered Him and said, 'Lord, if it is You, command me to come to You on the water.' So He said, 'Come.' And when Peter had come down out of the boat, he walked on the water to go to Jesus. But when he saw that the wind was boisterous, he was afraid; and beginning to sink he cried out, saying, 'Lord, save me!' And immediately Jesus stretched out His hand and caught him, and said to him, 'O you of little faith, why did you doubt?'"* In **Numbers 13:27, 28:30-33**, and **14:1-3**, ten out of twelve returning spies who were sent to Canaan brought back a fearful report that the giants in the promised land could make it very difficult to conquer. The result? An unavoidable 40 years of setback in claiming the Promised Land. However, Caleb and Joshua stood their ground to ensure that they claimed and conquered the Promised Land.

9. Lack of total belief in God could cause untold fear, as confirmed in **Isaiah 7:9b**, *"The head of Ephraim is Samaria, And the head of Samaria is Remaliah's son. If you will not believe, Surely you shall not be established."*

10. On most occasions, according to **Job 3:25**, the things that we usually fear or are afraid of are the very things that happen to us. The golden portion says, *"for the thing which I greatly feared is come upon me and that which I was afraid of is come unto me."* Hence a true child of God must endeavour to avoid fear as much as possible.

11. Undue anxiety can kill or cause unwarranted adverse effects on our health. This is exemplified in **Philippians 4:6-7**, *"Be anxious*

for nothing, but in everything by prayer and supplication, with thanksgiving, let your requests be made known to God; and the peace of God, which surpasses all understanding, will guard your hearts and minds through Christ Jesus."

12. Whatever Jesus says He will do or promises, He will surely do because He does not lie, according to **Numbers 23:19**, *"God is not a man, that He should lie, Nor a son of man, that He should repent. Has He said, and will He not do? Or has He spoken, and will He not make it good?"*

13. Our Lord is utterly capable of doing everything. **Jeremiah 32:27**, *"Behold, I am the Lord, the God of all flesh. Is there anything too hard for Me?",* **Philippians 4:13**, *"I can do all things through Christ who strengthens me."* **Psalm 55:22**, *"Cast your burden on the Lord, And He shall sustain you; He shall never permit the righteous to be moved."*

14. Fear can inevitably emerge whenever we endeavour to do things by relying on our energy, wisdom or imagination, and the holy book is unambiguous about it. In **Psalm 127:1**, the Bible says, *"Unless the Lord builds the house, They labor in vain who build it; Unless the Lord guards the city, The watchman stays awake in vain."* Also, **1 Samuel 2:9b** says, *"...But the wicked shall be silent in darkness. 'For by strength no man shall prevail.'"*

15. It is very profitable to believe and obey His word without any doubt totally, and the Bible is very clear about this. In **2 Chronicles 20:20**, the Bible says, *"So they rose early in the morning and went out into the Wilderness of Tekoa; and as they went out, Jehoshaphat stood and said, 'Hear me, O Judah and you inhabitants of Jerusalem: Believe in the Lord your God, and you shall be established; believe His prophets, and you shall prosper.'"*

    In **Matthew 7:24-25**, the Bible says, *"Therefore whoever hears these sayings of Mine, and does them, I will liken him to a wise man who* *built his house on the rock: and the rain descended, the floods came, and the winds blew and beat on that house; and it did not fall, for it was founded on the rock."*

16. It is always profitable to rely on and keep our eyes on the promises of God through his only son, Jesus Christ of Nazareth, as shown in **2 Timothy 1:12b**, *"...for I know whom I have believed and am persuaded that He is able to keep what I have committed to Him until that Day"* and **Hebrews 12:2a & 3b**, *"... looking unto Jesus, the author and finisher of our faith..."* and *"...lest you become weary and discouraged in your souls."*

17. On several occasions, I have confirmed that many people develop fear because of what others might say, feel, or think. In some circumstances, they even become ashamed in case of eventual failure, and it is quite erroneous indeed.

5

Why Must I Cheer up?

According to this book's title, "cheer up, don't despair," it is always advisable for humans to let go of depression, aggression, riffs, anger, quarrelsomeness, fighting, dullness, and any form of emotional imbalance.

Each and any one of the above could easily pave the way for hypertension, sudden death, illness, calamity, or even frequent doctor visits. It is advisable for us to be cheerful as much as possible because it is better for our general welfare. Many people hardly smile because they find it difficult to do so. A lot of medical practitioners have advised that one must, as a matter of compulsion, laugh as much as possible on a daily basis.

Biblically, we are cautioned to rely solely on God and gain total trust in some Golden Verses, as shown below, because He wants us to remain comforted at all times, as much as possible:

1. **Psalm 91:1-2** - *"He who dwells in the secret place of the Most High Shall abide under the shadow of the Almighty. I will say of the Lord, 'He is my refuge and my fortress; My God, in Him I will trust.'"*

2. His love is everlasting, and He cares for us, His children, according to **Psalm 103:8-18**.
3. He is our unfailing shepherd, according to **Psalm 23**. Every verse of this popular and widely read psalm means a lot and has a resounding interpretation.
4. **Deuteronomy 32:10-12** says, *"He found him in a desert land And in the wasteland, a howling wilderness; He encircled him, He instructed him, He kept him as the apple of His eye. As an eagle stirs up its nest, hovers over its young, Spreading out its wings, taking them up, Carrying them on its wings, So the Lord alone led him, And there was no foreign god with him."* In other words, God diligently cares for His own without fail.
5. Unknown to us, God works everything together for our good, as confirmed in **Romans 8:28**, *"And we know that all things work together for good to those who love God, to those who are called according to His purpose."*
6. His grace is sufficient for our needs. **2 Corinthians 9:8**, *"And God is able to make all grace abound toward you, that you, always having all sufficiency in all things, may have an abundance for every good work."* Imagine the thorn in the flesh of Paul. Yet God said His grace is sufficient for him because His power is made perfect in weakness, according to **2 Corinthians 12:9**, *"And He said to me, 'My grace is sufficient for you, for My strength is made perfect in weakness.' Therefore most gladly I will rather boast in my infirmities, that the power of Christ may rest upon me."*
7. Our heavenly Father is the source of all comfort, based on the contents of **2 Corinthians 1:3-4**, *"Blessed be the God and Father of our Lord Jesus Christ, the Father of mercies and God of all comfort, who comforts us in all our tribulation, that we may be able to comfort those who are in any trouble, with the comfort with which we ourselves are comforted by God."*

8. With His commitment to supply our needs according to His glorious riches in Christ Jesus (**Philippians 4:19**), a true child of God needs not to fear but be cheerful at all times.
9. His unfailing power can turn weeping to everlasting joy or laughter within a short while, as popularly reflected in **Psalm 30:4-5**, *"Sing praise to the Lord, you saints of His, And give thanks at the remembrance of His holy name. For His anger is but for a moment, His favor is for life; Weeping may endure for a night, But joy comes in the morning."*
10. Through His infinite wisdom, God has a way of directing all things in all manners that transcend human understanding, knowledge or wisdom, according to **Romans 11:33-36**, and I quote, *"Oh, the depth of the riches both of the wisdom and knowledge of God! How unsearchable are His judgments and His ways past finding out! 'For who has known the mind of the Lord? Or who has become His counselor?' 'Or who has first given to Him And it shall be repaid to him?' For of Him and through Him and to Him are all things, to whom be glory forever. Amen."*
11. If God can care for the birds and the flowers, which are not fashioned after His image, then we should have nothing to fear but be cheerful at all times. In **Matthew 6:25-34**, with particular reference to verse 26, the Bible records: *"Look at the birds of the air, for they neither sow nor reap nor gather into barns; yet your heavenly Father feeds them. Are you not of more value than they?"* We must always bear in mind that the offspring of a dog is always a dog; a sheep gives birth to a sheep, while a lion can never deliver an elephant! No wonder the Bible accentuates that since we are children of God, we are also gods, based on **Psalm 82:6**!
12. Just imagine how God ensured that Elijah never went without food nor water during the famine in Israel because of how he wholeheartedly trusted in the Lord. **(1 Kings 17:1-24)** Picture the miraculous way with which He used ordinary ravens to feed and

take care of Elijah was told by God that *"You will drink from the brook and I have ordered the ravens to feed you there."* Elijah went to the Kerith Brooklyn east of the Jordan and stayed there. The ravens brought him hot bread and meat in the morning and the evening, and he drank from the brook!

13. We must always remember that God is the Potter while we are the clay so He can decide to deal with us as He pleases. **Jeremiah 18:5-6** says, *"Then the word of the Lord came to me, saying: 'O house of Israel, can I not do with you as this potter?' says the Lord. 'Look, as the clay is in the potter's hand, so are you in My hand, O house of Israel!'"* Many people become disgruntled whenever they are facing challenges in life. However, the Bible admonishes us never to complain, as captured in **Isaiah 45:9-11**, and I quote: *"Woe to him who strives with his Maker! Let the potsherd strive with the potsherds of the earth! Shall the clay say to him who forms it, 'What are you making?' Or shall your handiwork say, 'He has no hands'? Woe to him who says to his father, 'What are you begetting?' Or to the woman, 'What have you brought forth?' Thus says the Lord, the Holy One of Israel, and his Maker: 'Ask Me of things to come concerning My sons; And concerning the work of My hands, you command Me.'"*

14. Joseph gladly acknowledged God's supremacy and providence when he was sold into slavery in Egypt, as recorded in **Genesis 45:1-14**. Verses 4 to 8 really caught my fancy and are worth elaborating on: *"And Joseph said to his brothers, 'Please come near to me.' So they came near. Then he said: 'I am Joseph your brother, whom you sold into Egypt. But now, do not therefore be grieved or angry with yourselves because you sold me here; for God sent me before you to preserve life. For these two years the famine has been in the land, and there are still five years in which there will be neither plowing nor harvesting. And God sent me before you to preserve a posterity for you in the earth, and to save your lives by a great deliverance. So now it*

was not you who sent me here, but God; and He has made me a father to Pharaoh, and Lord of all his house, and a ruler throughout all the land of Egypt.'"* The above scenario is very apt as far as the title of this book is concerned. Why and how? Not many people would behave the way Joseph did in this "predicament," with equanimity. Most would have easily become disillusioned right from when Joseph was thrown into prison based on a false allegation by Potiphar's wife! He remained persistent as if he knew that he was just 12 hours away from the throne of success in life!

15. Whenever God gives someone a daunting task, He ensures that He goes with them, provided the person is openly steadfast, determined, focused, and resolute. **Deuteronomy 31:7-8** says, *"Then Moses called Joshua and said to him in the sight of all Israel, "Be strong and of good courage, for you must go with this people to the land which the Lord has sworn to their fathers to give them, and you shall cause them to inherit it. And the Lord, He is the One who goes before you. He will be with you, He will not leave you nor forsake you; do not fear nor be dismayed."* Again, God is emphasising the essence of doggedness against all odds in the face of any difficulties.

16. God sometimes allows us to experience moments of grief but simultaneously paves the way for unflinching mercy. **Lamentations 3:31-33** says, *"For the Lord will not cast off forever. Though He causes grief, Yet He will show compassion According to the multitude of His mercies. For He does not afflict willingly, Nor grieve the children of men."* Also, in **Lamentations 3:37-42**, the Bible says, *"Who is he who speaks and it comes to pass, When the Lord has not commanded it? Is it not from the mouth of the Most High That woe and well-being proceed? Why should a living man complain, a man for the punishment of his sins? Let us search out and examine our ways, and turn back to the Lord; Let us lift our hearts and hands To God in heaven. We have transgressed and rebelled; You have not pardoned."*

17. Sometimes, when we pass through tribulation, it is not because of our sins or misdeed, as shown in **John 9**. I strongly encourage you to find time to read and digest the story patiently. The summary of the man that was born blind, according to Jesus, was to proclaim God's glory and to win souls for Jesus Christ in the town! The case is similar to the Bible account of Paul's imprisonment in **Philippians 1:12-14**, which I wish to quote thus: *"But I want you to know, brethren, that the things which happened to me have actually turned out for the furtherance of the gospel, so that it has become evident to the whole palace guard, and to all the rest, that my chains are in Christ; and most of the brethren in the Lord, having become confident by my chains, are much more bold to speak the word without fear."*

18. God's sovereignty can never be challenged by mortal beings. The following Golden Verses will inspire you:

- **Proverbs 21:30** – *"There is no wisdom or understanding Or counsel against the Lord."*
- **Psalm 135:6** – *"Whatever the Lord pleases He does, in heaven and in earth, in the seas and in all deep places."*
- **Proverbs 16:9** – *"A man's heart plans his way, But the Lord directs his steps."*

Worry and anxiety can shorten one's life. Things may occasionally be tough, and you may not be where you want to be, but just trust and obey God. Tomorrow will surely be better.

- **John 14:1** – *"Let not your heart be troubled; you believe in God, believe also in Me."*

Don't be like Naomi in the book of Ruth 1:19-21, *"Now the two of them went until they came to Bethlehem. And it happened, when they had*

come to Bethlehem, that all the city was excited because of them; and the women said, 'is this Naomi?' But she said to them, 'Do not call me Naomi; call me Mara, for the Almighty has dealt very bitterly with me. I went out full, and the Lord has brought me home again empty. Why do you call me Naomi, since the Lord has testified against me, and the Almighty has afflicted me?'"
Can I ask you something? What are those things which are bothering you and disturbing you like Naomi?

Take them to God instead of being saddened by such events. Go into your prayer closet and take your supplications to God with fasting. Support such with personal vigils and powerful Golden Verses to drive them home.

Don't ever forget: **cheer up, don't despair**.

19. **Proverbs 12:25** – *"Anxiety in the heart of man causes depression, But a good word makes it glad."*
20. **Proverbs 17:22** – *"A merry heart does good, like medicine, But a broken spirit dries the bones."*

6

Major Causes of Despair

As mentioned earlier, despair could be a build-up from aggression, low self-esteem or low morale arising from a prior incident or occurrence. However, one major cause of despair is depression. It could be spiritual, physical, or even both, depending on the victim's strength in Christ or moral standing. What then are the things that could give rise to depression? Let us examine some of them:

1. **Inability to sincerely confess our sins:** A good case in point was that of David, the psalmist. After he committed adultery with Bathsheba, he became uncomfortable, as shown in Psalm 32:3-4, where he said, *"When I kept silent, my bones wasted away through my groaning all day long. For day and night, Your hand was heavy upon me, my strength was sapped in the heat of summer."*

2. **Following the above, sincere confession becomes inevitable; we must therefore seek God's forgiveness:** Verse 5 of the same Psalm above says, *"Then I acknowledged my sin to You and did not cover up my iniquity. I said, 'I will confess my transgressions to the Lord,' and You forgave the guilt of my sin."*

3. **Guilty is entirely unavoidable if we fail to realize our sins and confess them to God:** Cain is a vivid example here, as recorded in Genesis 4:6-7, *"So the Lord said to Cain, 'Why are you angry? And why has your countenance fallen? If you do well, will you not be accepted? And if you do not do well, sin lies at the door. And its desire is for you, but you should rule over it.'"*

4. **Many people do not put their hope in God:** Whenever they are downcast or have any challenge, they run helter-skelter to other human beings instead of running to the greatest physician and the unchangeable Changer that never fails. See Psalm 46:5-6, *"God is in the midst of her, she shall not be moved; God shall help her, just at the break of dawn. The nations raged, the kingdoms were moved; He uttered His voice, the earth melted."*

5. **Many people are just nervous due to fearfulness.**

6. **Some people are easily worried over very simple or petty matters that should ordinarily be overlooked or ignored.** Psalm 118:6, *"The Lord is on my side; I will not fear. What can man do to me?"* Proverbs 29:25, *"The fear of man brings a snare, But whoever trusts in the Lord shall be safe."* Jeremiah 1:8, *"Do not be afraid of their faces, For I am with you to deliver you,' says the Lord."* Ezekiel 3:9b puts this point more succinctly, *"Yet, if you warn the wicked, and he does not turn from his wickedness, nor from his wicked way, he shall die in his iniquity; but you have delivered your soul."*

7. **Fear, despair or depression could be experienced if our hearts begin to tremble, which can even reflect on our hands:** Job 4:14, *"Fear came upon me, and trembling, Which made all my bones shake."*

8. **It is essential for a true child of God to establish the source of the devil's attacks, lies, and fears that could cause despair or depression:** We are, however, advised not to give any space to the devil, according to Ephesians 4:27 says, *"nor give*

place to the devil." Similarly, James 4:7, *"Therefore submit to God. Resist the devil and he will flee from you."*

9. **As true children of the Most High God, we must always strive to know that we are not supposed to be afraid, that we are righteous before Him and can beat our chests, knowing that He is on our side:** In Joshua 1:9, God told Joshua, *"Have I not commanded you? Be strong and of good courage; do not be afraid, nor be dismayed, for the Lord your God is with you wherever you go."* Many Believers occasionally forget that eternal salvation is guaranteed in Christ Jesus, but it has to be fully activated regularly. Isaiah 12:2, *"Behold, God is my salvation, I will trust and not be afraid; 'For Yah, the Lord, is my strength and song; He also has become my salvation.'"* Isaiah 26:3, *"You will keep him in perfect peace, Whose mind is stayed on You, Because he trusts in You."*

10. **Iniquity or deliberate instability of our ways causes many of us to occasionally fail to realize or forget that we are not supposed to experience nightmares under any circumstance:** This assurance can be found in some of the highlighted references below: Proverbs 3:24, *"When you lie down, you will not be afraid; Yes, you will lie down and your sleep will be sweet."* Psalm 4:8, *"I will both lie down in peace, and sleep; For You alone, O Lord, make me dwell in safety."* 2 Timothy 1:7, *"For God has not given us a spirit of fear, but of power and of love and of a sound mind."*

11. **Bad dreams are the reason why some people become despondent:** Many bad dreams arise or occur just to frighten us because they are spiritually meaningless, as confirmed in Ecclesiastes 5:7, *"For in the multitude of dreams and many words there is also vanity. But fear God."*

12. **Prayer is always the master key, and many children of God hardly find time to pray, and if they do, it is usually**

casual prayer instead of deep-rooted, Spirit-filled, demon-shaking prayer:** Hear what the Bible says in the following references: Psalm 34:4, *"I sought the Lord, and He heard me, And delivered me from all my fears."* Matthew 18:19, *"Again I say to you that if two of you agree on earth concerning anything that they ask, it will be done for them by My Father in heaven."* Psalm 42:8, *"The Lord will command His loving-kindness in the daytime, And in the night His song shall be with me— A prayer to the God of my life."* John 14:27, *"Peace I leave with you, My peace I give to you; not as the world gives do I give to you. Let not your heart be troubled, neither let it be afraid."*

13. **The majority of our youth, who form a greater part of the population of most countries, develop depression due to peer pressure:** The Bible cautions us boldly against this, according to Exodus 23:2, *"You shall not follow a crowd to do evil; nor shall you testify in a dispute so as to turn aside after many to pervert justice."*

14. **We must always put God first in all circumstances and at all costs:** Micah 7:5-7, *"Do not trust in a friend; do not put your confidence in a companion; Guard the doors of your mouth from her who lies in your bosom."* Romans 12:2 explains it more potently, *"And do not be conformed to this world, but be transformed by the renewing of your mind, that you may prove what is that good and acceptable and perfect will of God."*

7

Fear Demystified

A lot of people battle serious fears in many areas of their lives, which could include:

1. **Fear of poverty**
2. **Fear of being raped**
3. **Fear of being molested in one form or the other**
4. **Fear of being robbed**
5. **Fear of being cheated on**
6. **Fear of being divorced by one's spouse**
7. **Fear of having the fruit of the womb**
8. **Fear of having road accidents**
9. **Fear of failure**
10. **Fear of being cheated in a business venture, especially in the case of a proposed partnership**
11. **Fear of sudden death**

Many people put themselves in perpetual bondage or a terrifying state of despair when they have a bad dream one night and begin to exercise unwarranted distress before or whenever they are about to go to bed. Why? They are afraid of having "another bitter experience or spiritual attack through a bad dream."

It is unfortunate that many souls have surrendered their lives to fear, which basically arose due to doubt. It is also unfortunate that once some people encounter any little disappointment, rejection or suppression in one area of their lives, they easily become glued to the negative, or shall I say, the tendency to believe that it shall become the norm in their life.

Unbeknownst to them, they have indirectly opened the gates for fear and despair, which ordinarily should not have come into their lives in the first place. Once fear is given a warehouse in one's life, it will unavoidably cripple good and rightful thinking, suppress brilliant ideas, and hinder the performance of the Holy Spirit in one's life, which could ultimately lead to backwardness retardation and slow growth.

Many people do not know that fear or despair is a state of mind constantly being determined by negative spirits. Jesus Christ dominates the positive angle, while the devil encourages and nurtures the negative aspect. Whoever lives a sinful life will constantly be haunted by a guilty conscience even without anything pursuing them in the first place!

On the contrary, if anyone strives hard to live their life according to God's tenets, rules, statutes, and commandments, Jesus will always control the person's ship. Thus, while the former will always be under the influence of fear, the latter is bound to enjoy God's unrestricted freedom to enjoy a fearless life.

Conversely, many people are usually under the terrible attack of demons, which could arise due to several reasons:

1. **Satanic attacks in their dreams**
2. **Unwarranted attacks due to jealousy**

3. **Perpetual demonic or spiritual attacks**
4. **Generational or family-related attacks due to curses**
5. **Attacks due to marital matters or issues**

We can safely conclude that as a child of God who abides by His laws, our faith is always expected to be active so that we can live a fearless life.

On the other hand, those who constantly commit sins and do not live as children of God are of the devil, and he is free to dominate their lives with perpetual fear, which makes them vulnerable to his dominion over them. Fear gives way for the devil to enter, and if care is not taken to quickly dislodge it from one's life, he could continue to dominate the person's life.

How do we Guard Against it?

The Bible is replete with very powerful scriptures that can be applied to deal with this. Herein comes the aspect of our mind and our mouth, especially the words that come out of our hearts.

As soon as we begin to experience the presence of negative spirits in our hearts, the next most important thing to be done is to begin to declare the word of God, as enshrined in the Bible, which is the best Christian manual in the world!

Did anyone say that you will die, or has a negative pronouncement been made concerning your family or loved ones? You must immediately begin to declare God's scriptures to cancel, reverse, or blot it out, with abounding faith as shown in the following scriptures:

1. **Isaiah 10:27** – *"It shall come to pass in that day That his burden will be taken away from your shoulder, And his yoke from your neck, And the yoke will be destroyed because of the anointing oil."*
2. **1 Peter 2:24** – *"...who Himself bore our sins in His own body on the tree, that we, having died to sins, might live for righteousness— by whose stripes you were healed."*
3. **Isaiah 28:18** – *"Your covenant with death will be annulled, And your agreement with Sheol will not stand; When the overflowing scourge passes through, Then you will be trampled down by it."*
4. **Psalm 34:19** – *"Many are the afflictions of the righteous, But the Lord delivers him out of them all."* Above all, we must always remember that since God used the spoken Word to bring the world into being and because we are gods like Him (Psalm 82:6), we can equally use our mouths profitably to declare powerful statements that can remain permanent.
5. **Proverbs 18:21** and **23:7** both state that the power of life and death are in the tongue
6. **Romans 10:17** - *"Faith cometh by hearing and hearing by the word of God."*

Those who are steadfast and walk in Christ with constant faith have nothing to fear as long as they regularly declare God's words to dispel doubts and negative tendencies.

A much fitting example is the COVID-19 epidemic, which is now trending worldwide. It is wrecking most economies of the world, and as a result, many people have lost their main sources of livelihood. Despite being people of faith, if someone keeps telling us that we will continue to be in abject poverty, we should constantly refute this by claiming the contents of Genesis 26:12-14, where the Bible says that despite the famine in the land, Israel was living a very prosperous life to the extent that He was lending to some of the nations of the world.

Philippians 4:19 is another relevant special scripture that must be relied on, which says, *"My God shall supply all your needs according to His riches and glory by Christ Jesus."*

Remember, Romans 8:15 says, *"For ye have not received the spirit of fear... ABBA father,"* and Jesus has said that He will never leave us nor forsake us (Hebrews 13:15). The concept is similar in Colossians 1:27, *"Christ in us, the hope of glory."*

I came across the book of Isaiah, chapter 43:1-7 at the age of 12, which appropriately contains God's powerful assurances that He will always be with us, whether we are passing through waters, rivers or even fire. This promise is repeated throughout the entire contents of Psalms 20, 27, 46, 91, 121, and 125. I strongly encourage you to pray and claim these contents always.

If we allow the devil to penetrate our hearts and begin to proclaim negative words or testimonies without rebuking them, they will come to stay and remain permanently in our lives, as found in Romans 10:10.

A vivid example was when God allowed the devil to tempt Job. In Job 3:25, Job said, *"For the thing which I greatly feared is upon me and that which I was afraid of is come on to me."* So, we must constantly eradicate the spirit of fear from our lives.

8

What Must we do?

Many people have unavoidably found themselves intricately bound by the spirit of fear because they always want to satisfy or please their fellow beings instead of believing in the Supreme Being. Many have also lost their self-confidence because they constantly allow other people's perceptions of them to dominate their daily activities. They tend to forget the contents of Galatians 1:10, which says, *"For do I now persuade men, or God? Or do I seek to please men? For if I still pleased men, I would not be a bondservant of Christ."*

Many people also fail to realize that there are always two sides to a coin. No country's currency has only one side, whether paper or coin. Similarly, there are usually two opposing aspects to life, such as:

1. **Faith and fear**
2. **Life and death**
3. **Good and bad**
4. **Good and evil**
5. **Male and female**
6. **Front and back**

7. **Beautiful and ugly**
8. **Awake and asleep**
9. **Come and go**
10. **Rich and poor**
11. **Up and down**
12. **Light and darkness**
13. **Morning and night**
14. **Success and failure**
15. **God and the devil**

Why the above analogy? Plain and simple. At every point in our lives, there are always two forces that operate within our subconscious mind, whether we believe it or not! And whether we like it or not, it is the one that we yield to that has or gains the upper hand in dominating our life, destiny or mood. That is why it was recorded in the Bible that "by two or more witnesses, a thing is established."

Deuteronomy 19:15 - *"One witness shall not rise against a man concerning any iniquity or any sin that he commits; by the mouth of two or three witnesses the matter shall be established."*

2 Corinthians 13:1 – *"This will be the third time I am coming to you. 'By the mouth of two or three witnesses every word shall be established.'"*

Amos 3:3 – *"Can two walk together, unless they are agreed?"*

Matthew 18:26 – *"The servant therefore fell down before him, saying, 'Master, have patience with me, and I will pay you all.'"*

If we give room to what the devil is drumming into our ears, hearts or life, it is bound to be negative in nature and content and has the potential to create fear and destructive imaginations in our lives. Therefore, we must strive to avoid negative ideas and thinking because they could lead to destruction, losses, depression, and calamity if utmost care is not taken.

As a true image of God, Jeremiah 29:11 must constantly stare us in the face, permanently reflect in our hearts, and be our daily reference point. Have you come across it before? Listen to this, *"For I know the thoughts that I think towards you,' says the Lord, 'thoughts of peace and not of evil, to give you an expected end.'"*

We must endeavour to hold onto the above promises as much as possible. If God has said it, it is left for us to claim it and always allow God's positive spirits to minister to our innermost being. The choice is ultimately ours.

Let me bring in a very logical and practical example here. Although God promised the children of Israel that they would enter the Promised Land, they still had challenges along the way. Shortly before they got there, Moses selected twelve men to go as spies to the land. Only two of them gave encouraging reports, while the other ten said it was impossible to go and occupy the land. Caleb and Joshua were those two, but it was Caleb, full of faith, high spirits and boldness that said, *"Let us go out once and possess it because we can overcome it,"* according to Numbers 13:30. On the contrary, the other ten said they saw giants and men of great stature, as recorded in Numbers 13:31-32 and 14:1. Obviously, Caleb displayed a high level of faith because even though he also saw the occupants of the land as Anaks and giants, he did not allow their looks and stature to intimidate him, unlike the other ten!

It is proper for me to safely conclude that whenever we are able to safely extricate fear, despair can never find a place to thrive in our lives, timidity would flee, doubt would have no place to grow, and the ultimate situation for us as believers would be to remain cheerful, all the days of our lives.

9

Final Antidotes & Nuggets for Fear

From all that we have discussed so far in this book, let me attempt to summarize as follows:

1. **As true children of God, we must learn to live a righteous life in order to be in alignment with God's principles.**
2. **We must always think right by banishing negative thoughts from our hearts, minds and ears.**
3. **We must realize that everybody has guardian angels who must be put to work at all times:** Psalm 34:7, *"The angel of the Lord encamps all around those who fear Him, And delivers them."* 2 Kings 6:16 – *"So he answered, 'Do not fear, for those who are with us are more than those who are with them.'"* It is essential for us to believe that our angels are always with us because Jesus Christ said in John 20:29, *"Blessed are those who have not seen but they believe."* A true child of God must be able to claim the authority in Psalm 91:11, *"For He shall give His angels charge over you, to keep you in all your ways."*

4. **As believers, we must acquaint ourselves with the word of God and constantly apply it to our lives to dispel and ward off negative thoughts, spirits, and devilish incantations:** We must also diligently guard what we say. 2 Timothy 1:7, *"For God has not given us a spirit of fear, but of power and of love and of a sound mind."*

5. **We must constantly bear in mind that two forces are constantly in operation, which must challenge us to hook onto the positive force regularly:** The force of the devil relates to sin and death (hence, we must refrain from living a sinful life). The force of God relates to living a righteous life that radiates and emits the spirit of life in Christ Jesus. Doubt must never be allowed to occupy any aspect of our lives. Psalm 118:27, *"God is the Lord, And He has given us light; Bind the sacrifice with cords to the horns of the altar."* Proverbs 18:21, *"Death and life are in the power of the tongue, And those who love it will eat its fruit."*

6. **We must constantly remind ourselves that diving protection and permanent salvation are ours:** Hebrews 13:5, *"Let your conduct be without covetousness; be content with such things as you have. For He Himself has said, 'I will never leave you nor forsake you.'"* I don't want to occupy this book with the entire passage of Isaiah 41:10-13, but it is a wonderful portion of the scriptures that I came across during my very first trip outside of my home country to the United Kingdom in June 1978. I encourage you to familiarize yourself with it and begin to pray using it as much as possible, as frequently as possible.

7. **Never allow any situation to reduce or diminish your self-confidence or boldness in God:** Your self-esteem must always be growing from strength to strength. Men may want to reject you or disapprove of your line of thinking, but as long as you believe in yourself and you believe you are in right-standing with the tenets of God, be bold in Christ and look upright at all times.

8. **You must be unwavering whenever you are making decisions:** Always allow God's Divine Spirit to dwell in you and guide your steps. Psalm 118:6, *"The Lord is on my side; I will not fear. What can man do to me?"*
9. **Allow the Holy Spirit to totally engulf your daily activities:** Isaiah 61:1, *"The Spirit of the Lord God is upon Me, Because the Lord has anointed Me To preach good tidings to the poor; He has sent Me to heal the brokenhearted, to proclaim liberty to the captives, And the opening of the prison to those who are bound..."*
10. **Never harbour hatred towards anybody. No matter the reason, always keep an open mind.**
11. **Endeavour to live as a true child of God and reflect His image in your thoughts, deeds, mode of expression, speech, and watch what you listen to.**
12. **Move with the right type of people. Choose your friends carefully:** There are two very popular English proverbs that say, "Show me your friend, and I will show you who you are," and "Birds of the same feather, congregate together."
13. **Despair can never dominate our lives if we constantly eliminate fear from our lives.**
14. **Once fear and despair are effectively checkmated from our lives, joy, happiness, and undiluted dominion in the Holy Spirit become our birthright for life.**

10

Why Must we Cheer up?

As I conclude this book, I consider it pertinent to quickly highlight reasons to endeavour to be cheerful.

Before I make brief scripture references, being careful is far much better than looking dejected, worried, disturbed, or worn out due to one reason or the other.

Some people find it extremely difficult or unnecessary to smile, let alone laugh. Some will just tighten their faces throughout the day, irrespective of the number of good things surrounding them. Medical doctors encourage human beings to smile as often as possible daily because it gives us a positive boost to the face and equally supports longevity. I have also heard the same advice during a Health and Welfare seminar during one of my trips to West Germany in March 1987 and have been applying the advice since then.

Those who frown their faces inadvertently drive people away from them. People may not be very comfortable moving close to them, let alone trying to do any tangible business with them. That could invariably force people to withhold vital and valuable information from them that could be of great benefit, which is unsafe and perhaps dangerous.

Many parents do not create a friendly or conducive environment for their children to be free with them. Such children find it convenient to find solace in speaking their minds and derive great joy by discussing their intimate and personal issues with other people outside their family. This is not right. Such children could be misled by third parties simply because they cannot approach their biological parents for any heart-to-heart discussion.

Some bosses at work are always difficult to approach because of their stance and posture, which would make it quite uneasy for junior staff to approach them with anything that could be useful. I have a lot of examples that I could easily cite, but I wish to mention Biblical references that confirm the fact that it is always better to be cheerful at all times instead of being despondent, unhappy, or scorn-faced:

1. **Proverbs 15:14** – *"The heart of him who has understanding seeks knowledge, But the mouth of fools feeds on foolishness."*
2. **Acts 24:10** – *"Then Paul, after the governor had nodded to him to speak, answered: 'Inasmuch as I know that you have been for many years a judge of this nation, I do the more cheerfully answer for myself...'"*
3. **2 Corinthians 9:7** – *"So let each one give as he purposes in his heart, not grudgingly or of necessity; for God loves a cheerful giver."*
4. **Romans 12:8** – *"...he who exhorts, in exhortation; he who gives, with liberality; he who leads, with diligence; he who shows mercy, with cheerfulness."*
5. **Psalm 68:3** – *"But let the righteous be glad; Let them rejoice before God; Yes, let them rejoice exceedingly."*

6. **Psalm 118:24** – *"This is the day the Lord has made; We will rejoice and be glad in it."*
7. **Proverbs 15:30** – *"The light of the eyes rejoices the heart, And a good report makes the bones healthy."*
8. **Proverbs 17:22** – *"A merry heart does good, like medicine, But a broken spirit dries the bones."*
9. **James 5:13** – *"Is anyone among you suffering? Let him pray. Is anyone cheerful? Let him sing psalms."*
10. **Galatians 5:22-26** – *"But the fruit of the Spirit is love, joy, peace, longsuffering, kindness, goodness, faithfulness, gentleness, self-control. Against such there is no law. And those who are Christ's have crucified the flesh with its passions and desires. If we live in the Spirit, let us also walk in the Spirit. Let us not become conceited, provoking one another, envying one anyone."*
11. **Luke 6:22-23** – *"Blessed are you when men hate you, And when they exclude you, And revile you, and cast out your name as evil, For the Son of Man's sake. Rejoice in that day and leap for joy! For indeed your reward is great in heaven, For in like manner their fathers did to the prophets."*
12. **James 1:2-3** – *"My brethren, count it all joy when you fall into various trials, knowing that the testing of your faith produces patience."*
13. **Psalm 4:6-8** – *"There are many who say, 'Who will show us any good?' Lord, lift up the light of Your countenance upon us. You have put gladness in my heart, More than in the season that their grain and wine increased. I will both lie down in peace, and sleep; For You alone, O Lord, make me dwell in safety."*
14. **Philippians 4:4-5** – *"Rejoice in the Lord always. Again I will say, rejoice! Let your gentleness be known to all men. The Lord is at hand."*
15. **Jude 1:2-5** – *"Mercy, peace, and love be multiplied to you. Beloved, while I was very diligent to write to you concerning our common*

salvation, I found it necessary to write to you exhorting you to contend earnestly for the faith which was once for all delivered to the saints. For certain men have crept in unnoticed, who long ago were marked out for this condemnation, ungodly men, who turn the grace of our God into lewdness and deny the only Lord God and our Lord Jesus Christ. But I want to remind you, though you once knew this, that the Lord, having saved the people out of the land of Egypt, afterward destroyed those who did not believe."

16. **Psalm 47:1-3** – *"Oh, clap your hands, all you peoples! Shout to God with the voice of triumph! For the Lord Most High is awesome; He is a great King over all the earth. He will subdue the peoples under us, And the nations under our feet."*

17. **Psalm 97:10-12** – *"You who love the Lord, hate evil! He preserves the souls of His saints; He delivers them out of the hand of the wicked. Light is sown for the righteous, And gladness for the upright in heart. Rejoice in the Lord, you righteous, And give thanks at the remembrance of His holy name."*

Finally, as you've read this book, endeavour to recommend it to your loved ones and put what you have read into practice.

Meditate and pray with the cited Golden verses as often as possible. Watch your speech, avoid doubts and build up your confidence level regularly. Never entertain fear under any circumstances, and be conscious of your guardian angel.

It is well with you forever. Amen.

A Sinner's Prayer

Dear Heavenly Father,

I come to You in the Name of Jesus Christ.

You said in Your Word, "Whosoever shall call upon the name of the Lord shall be saved" (Romans 10:13). I am calling on Your Name, so I know You have saved me now.

You also said that "if you confess with your mouth the Lord Jesus and believe in your heart that God has raised Him from the dead, you will be saved. For with the heart one believes unto righteousness, and with the mouth, confession is made unto salvation" (Romans 10:9-10). I believe in my heart Jesus Christ is the Son of God. I believe that He was raised from the dead for my justification, and I confess Him now as my Lord and Savior.

Thank you, Lord, because now, I am saved!

Thank You, Lord, because I know you have heard my prayer. Thank You, Lord, because I am now born again.

Signed _____

Date _____

About the Author

Apostle Dr. Victor Adekunle Adewusi was a passionate Spiritual Leader and Father of many children and grandchildren.

He was also the Author of five books "*The Secrets of Happy Parenting,*" "*Control Your Anger,*" "*Praise, Appreciation & Thanksgiving (PAT),*" "*Mine Shall Be Done,*" and "*Fear Not, Cheer Up, Do Not Despair.*"

Until his passing, he was the General Overseer of The Eternal Sacred Order of The Cherubim and Seraphim Church, Oke Ibukun Branco; The Governor of the Yabatech Class of 1986 governing council; a Member of The Chartered Institute of Management; A Fellow of The Chartered Institute of Taxation of Nigeria and A Fellow of The Institute of Chartered Accountants of Nigeria (ICAN).

Apostle Dr. Victor Adekunle, who was a philanthropist, has drawn on his personal breakthrough life experiences to help people overcome challenges and attain greater achievements in their life.

CPSIA information can be obtained
at www.ICGtesting.com
Printed in the USA
BVHW090332270822
645595BV00004B/503